Published in The United States of America
By Dr. Justin Imel, Roanoke, VA

Manufactured in The United States of America
First edition published 2015
Cover art and jacket design © 2015 Justin Imel

Author photo – Shawn Sprouse, SDS Photography,
Roanoke, VA

Accompanied by the Instruments of David

Examining Excuses for Instrumental Music in Worship

Dr. Justin Imel, Sr.

RJ&WC
Press

For

Aunt Thelma

Table of Contents

Introduction

Dad's mother honestly wished to honor God with her whole soul. She taught me so much about prayer and about service and about Bible study and about fearing God. She was a guiding light in my spiritual formation, and I miss the opportunity to call her often (even when I called using my cell phone, she wouldn't talk long – she just could never believe that long distance could really be free).

As much as I loved Mamaw and miss her sorely, my family sought not to be visiting on Sunday. Why? Because she worshiped at a church using mechanical instruments of music in worship and she became highly offended if we went elsewhere. I don't really like putting Mamaw's unbiblical worship practices in print – I don't wish to malign her in any way and I still have dear loved ones who worship incorrectly.

Mamaw taught Dad to worship improperly. Dad, who honestly and deeply loves the Lord, wanted to preach and bring souls to Jesus. He, therefore, went to a church-related school, a school affiliated with a group in error, to hone his preaching skills (and he's mighty good in the pulpit). Dad worked with a small church while in college and met and married my mother. Shortly upon marriage, Mom and Dad moved to eastern Kentucky where I could be born. The very first worship service I ever attended in this world had singing accompanied by mechanical instruments of music.

But, because my Dad loves the Lord and is honest, he spent time exploring God's truth. As Dad spent time in Scripture, he came to the only conclusion honest hearts will reach – God wishes to be praised with the human heart and voice without any other accompaniment. Dad has never looked back, and he has instilled in his three sons a desire to honor God as God wishes.

I share my family history to establish my credibility in writing this book. You see, I have heard every excuse under the sun to justify using instrumental music in public worship.

I don't enjoy sharing that family history, but I want to establish my credibility in writing this book. You see, I have heard every excuse under the sun to justify using instrumental music in public worship. When one examines those justifications in light of Scripture, they fail miserably. I'm not interested in your opinion (or mine, for that matter) – I wish to know what God says on the subject through his Word.

That Word from God must always be our guide. Holy "men spoke from God as they were carried along by the Holy Spirit" (2 Pet 1:21); the writers of Scripture didn't even give us their opinions – they gave us the Word of God. God blesses the one "who looks into the perfect law" and acts on what he reads (Js 1:25). In this book, we're striving to be among the blessed who look into God's Word and act on what they read.

Come along with me. Let's explore Scripture together and let us commit to following nothing but the Word of God. Soli Deo Gloria!

Roanoke, Virginia
November 19, 2015

1

Does It Really Matter?

I wouldn't be in this world were it not for instrumental music. Dad was preaching at Cornwell Christian Church in Frenchburg, Kentucky. The piano player told the preacher that she had this cute niece whom he needed to meet. The preacher and the piano player's niece met, and the rest is, as they say, history.

As I wrote in the introduction, instrumental music plays a large role in my personal history. Attending an a cappella congregation in my formative years and hearing Mamaw (and Dad for a number of years) say nothing was wrong with the instrument created tension in my heart over the issue. Thus, I spent time studying the instrumental music issue. As I studied what the Bible teaches, I heard people giving arguments against a cappella. One of the most frequent ideas I heard is that it really doesn't matter if we use the instrument or not – The New Testament never mentions instrumental music and, therefore, discussing instrumental music is barking up a tree God has not planted.

To buttress the argument that instrumental music is barking up the wrong tree, I've heard people say, "I really can't picture Jesus or Paul getting upset over whether or not a congregation used an instrument." Others have said, "Justin, do you really think that Jesus died on the cross to keep a piano out of a church service?"

With all due respect, emotional arguments do not change the fact that God has planted this tree. We need to think seriously about whether or not we use instrumental music in worship. God does care, and he has absolutely not given the decision about the use of instrumental music in worship to his people; instead, God wants a cappella singing and a cappella singing only.

Why does the instrumental music issue really matter?

One: The Sovereignty of God

Saying that God does not really care whether or not we use instrumental music in worship says that we – as worshipers of Jehovah God – may decide for ourselves how we worship. I know good people who understand God cares about certain aspects of worship – for example, worshiping on the first day of the week, male spiritual leadership, and partaking of the Eucharist – and I do not wish to malign them in any way whatsoever. Yet, if God cares about one or two aspects of worship, does not logic say that he cares about other parts of worship? In other words, why would God inspire instructions about the Eucharist and not singing or why would God command male spiritual leadership but give the decision of church music up to the worshiper?

If God really does not care how we worship, I would like to see much changed. My wife has great talent – I'd love to hear her preach (I do at home!), but 1 Timothy 2:8-15 prevents Tammy from preaching publicly. I honestly do not like the taste of unleavened bread; maybe I can make the Lord's Supper more palatable by substituting chocolate cake (I would love that!) – Jesus, however, used unleavened bread, and I have no authority in any way to change what Jesus did.

God has given me free will, and I may choose to act based on my own feelings, my own actions, and my own thoughts. But, simply because I can do something does not make that activity right.

"'All things are lawful for me,' but not all things are helpful" (1 Cor 6:12). The Corinthians had written a letter to Paul (1 Cor 7:1), and they apparently had written, "All things are lawful for me." They had an antinomian attitude – they threw off divine restraints and did whatever they wished. Paul corrects them in his Epistle; not everything I can do is helpful.

4

God is sovereign, and it is not up to me – or anyone else – to decide what we do religiously. God, and God alone, has the right to determine my worship, for he is sovereign.

God has great sovereignty in this world; he demonstrates that authority, for example, when he raises up kings and brings kings down. After Nebuchadnezzar boasted about the great Babylon he himself had built, a voice from heaven declares, "You shall be made to eat grass like an ox, and you shall be wet with the dew of heaven, and seven periods of time shall pass over you, till you know that the Most High rules the kingdom of men and gives it to whom he will" (Dan 4:25). Nebuchadnezzar had not made himself great; YWHW had made the emperor great. The Most High, not man, has sovereignty in this world.

I know you might be tempted to say, "Wait just a minute! God's sovereignty over Nebuchadnezzar shows that God has authority over the kingdoms of the world. You can't take such a text and apply that principle to worship." It's very true that Daniel 4 speaks of God's sovereignty over the Babylonian Empire.

However, if God has that much sovereignty over the nations of the world with their armies and weapons, think about the power he has over the rest of mankind. In fact, we know that God has such sovereignty. "The LORD reigns; he is robed in majesty; the LORD is robed; he has put on strength as his belt. Yes, the world is established; it shall never be moved. Your throne is established from of old; you are from everlasting" (Ps 93:1-2). "The LORD reigns; let the peoples tremble! He sits enthroned upon the cherubim; let the earth quake! The LORD is great in Zion; he is exalted over all the peoples. Let them praise your great and awesome name! Holy is he!" (Ps 99:1-3).

God also has sovereignty over the church. God "put all things under [Jesus'] feet and gave him as head over all things to the church, which is his body, the fullness of him who fills all in all" (Eph 1:22-23). How could God give Jesus

5

"as head over all things to the church" unless God is sovereign over the church? The church is often referenced as "the kingdom of God" in Scripture (e.g., Jn 18:36; Acts 8:12; Rom 14:17; Col 1:13). How can the church be "the kingdom of God" unless God is sovereign over the church?

God's reign, quite simply, means that God is in control and God has a right to tell me what to do. We like the idea of God's sovereignty when we're struggling – We might say that God is in control and all will turn out well. Yet, when I want control – when I want to do what I like – we find much more difficulty in seeing God as the One in control.

Regardless of what we might wish, God has used his sovereignty to instruct his people on worship. "The hour is coming, and is now here," says Jesus, "when the true worshipers will worship the Father in spirit and truth, for the Father is seeking such people to worship him. God is spirit, and those who worship him must worship in spirit and truth" (Jn 4:23-24). God, in his sovereignty, has not authorized his people to worship according to their own whims and desires, but he seeks those who will worship in "in spirit and truth."

God's sovereignty requires that I worship the Great I AM on his terms, not my own.

Two: The Standards of God

If it doesn't really matter whether or not I use instrumental music, God has not given man instructions for worship.

Man needs standards for worship in order to know how to honor God appropriately. "I know, O LORD, that the way of man is not in himself, that it is not in man who walks to direct his steps. Correct me, O LORD, but in justice; not in your anger, lest you bring me to nothing" (Jer 10:23-24). Notice that Jeremiah even asks God to correct him; if God has no standards, how could Jeremiah be corrected?

Some might object by saying that God indeed has

6

standards for the way we live, but he hasn't spoken on instrumental music in the New Testament; therefore, we can or cannot use the instrument at our own pleasure. In the Old Testament, God placed instrumental music under his sovereignty:

> The LORD spoke to Moses, saying, 'Make two silver trumpets. Of hammered work you shall make them, and you shall use them for summoning the congregation and for breaking camp . . . . On the day of your gladness also, and at your appointed feasts and at the beginnings of your months, you shall blow the trumpets over your burnt offerings and over the sacrifices of your peace offerings. They shall be a reminder of you before your God: I am the LORD your God" (Num 10:1-2, 10).

God regulated instrumental music in the tabernacle. Moses was commanded to make two silver trumpets. What if Moses had only made one? What if he had made three? What if Moses had made two golden trumpets? What if he had shaped them over a fire and not used a hammer? God specified that Moses was to make two silver trumpets of hammered work.

In fact, no other instrument was at any time authorized for worship in the tabernacle.

> Hezekiah "stationed the Levites in the house of the LORD with cymbals, harps, and lyres, according to the commandment of David and of Gad the king's seer and of Nathan the prophet, for the commandment was from the LORD through his prophets. The Levites stood with the instruments of David, and the priests with the trumpets. Then Hezekiah commanded that the burnt offering be offered on the altar. And when the burnt offering began, the song to the LORD began also, and the

trumpets, accompanied by the instruments of David king of Israel" (2 Chr 29:25-27).

In the temple, God commanded the use of cymbals, harps, and lyres, in addition to the use of the trumpets; the people had no choice in the use of these instruments, for God commanded their use. God never authorized any other instruments for temple worship. Other instruments were occasionally used in the worship of God: "Praise him with trumpet sound; praise him with lute and harp! Praise him with tambourine and dance; praise him with strings and pipe! Praise him with sounding cymbals; praise him with loud clashing cymbals!" (Ps 150:3-5). The Israelites used the lute and tambourine in worship, but they had no authority to use them in public worship – God never authorized them for public worship.

What do the commands given to the Israelites have to do with us today? God always specified what instrument was to be used. If God wanted instrumental music in modern worship, does it not stand to reason that he would have told us specifically what instrument to use?

Sometimes we hear that the New Testament is completely silent on the subject of instrumental music. Not so fast – The New Testament often mentions instrumental music. "Jesus came to the ruler's house and saw the flute players and the crowd making a commotion" (Matt 9:23ed). The Lord Jesus himself mentioned instrumental music – When speaking of the corrupt generation in which he dwelt, he said, "We played the flute for you, and you did not dance; we sang a dirge, and you did not weep" (Lk 7:32).

Paul mentioned instrumental music in his epistles. "If I speak in the tongues of men and of angels, but have not love, I am a noisy gong or a clanging cymbal" (1 Cor 13:1). "If even lifeless instruments, such as the flute or the harp, do not give distinct notes, how will anyone know what is played?" (1 Cor 14:7).

8

If Jesus and Paul discussed instrumental music, why did they never at any time mention instruments in connection with the praise of God? In other words, why did Jesus never say to his apostles, "Play the harp as you sing this hymn?" Why did Paul never say, "Sing and make melody in your hearts while someone makes music on the flute and someone else plays the cymbals?" If Jesus and his apostles were very well aware of instrumental music in society, would they not have mentioned that music in connection with God's praise if God desired such praise?

Three: The Severity of God

God has a long history of executing severe punishment upon those who worship inappropriately. The people of Israel had Aaron construct a golden calf while Moses was on Mt. Sinai (Ex 32). As a result of the people's sin, Moses instructed the sons of Levi to go throughout the camp and to kill their fellow Israelites. "The sons of Levi did according to the word of Moses. And that day about three thousand men of the people fell" (Ex 32:28). Yet, it seems that more than those three thousand men fell, for after that slaughter God says to Moses, "Lead the people to the place about which I have spoken to you; behold, my angel shall go before you. Nevertheless, in the day when I visit, I will visit their sin upon them" (Ex 23:34). Moses then records, "Then the LORD sent a plague on the people, because they made the calf, the one that Aaron made" (Ex 32:35). The New Testament also uses this episode as an example of false worship of God: "These things took place as examples for us, that we might not desire evil as they did. Do not be idolaters as some of them were; as it is written, 'The people sat down to eat and drink and rose up to play' [Ex 32:6]" (1 Cor 10:6-7).

In the Revelation, we read, "Then I heard a loud voice from the temple telling the seven angels, 'Go and pour out on the earth the seven bowls of the wrath of God.' So the first angel went and poured out his bowl on the earth, and harmful and painful sores came upon the people who bore the mark of the beast and *worshiped* its image" (Rev 16:1-2). The people of the earth worshiped the beast's image, and they paid a very high price for their improper worship.

Someone might object to those two examples by saying, "Justin, those examples both deal with idolatry, not the worship of the true God." Such a statement overlooks the fact that the golden calf was an example of the false worship of the true God. Notice what Aaron said after he constructed the calf: "These are your gods, O Israel, who brought you up out of the land of Egypt!" (Ex 32:5). The people were not worshiping a pagan deity, but they were worshiping YHWH in a way he did not desire. Even when there is pagan idolatry involved, the point is that God has said, "Here's how you worship," the people disregarded what God said, and God, therefore, punished.

Does God continue to punish those who worship inappropriately? You betcha! Notice what the author of Hebrews says, "Let us be grateful for receiving a kingdom that cannot be shaken, and thus let us offer to God acceptable worship, with reverence and awe" (Heb 12:28). The term for "acceptable" means to be well-pleasing to one.

Why should we offer to God acceptable worship? "For our God is a consuming fire" (Heb 12:29). As a consuming fire, God will extract vengeance on his enemies. In the context of Hebrews 12, those enemies upon whom the Lord God will exact vengeance are those who do not offer "acceptable worship, with reverence and awe."

Let us come to God with reverence and awe. Let us worship him as he desires, not as we might wish. It matters greatly whether or not we use instrumental music in worship. Let us honor God with our voices, not with lifeless instruments.

10

2

Psallō and the Piano

A preacher once told me about a robbery late one night at the church building. The alarm system notified both him and the police department. When the preacher arrived at the building, the sheriff had already arrived and was looking around. The sheriff looked at the preacher and said, "It doesn't look like they took anything but your piano!"

Indeed, we in the churches of Christ stand out among the religious world for using a cappella music in worship it's only right to mention that some other groups – Old Regular Baptist and the Amish, for example – also sing a cappella). People will occasionally look at us and say, "What's the big deal? It's just a nice aid to our singing?"

In a similar vein, we often hear that the Greek term *psallō* justifies instrumental music in worship. The word originally meant to pluck or to twang a bowstring. Ancient Greek authors and even the Greek Old Testament, the Septuagint, use *psallō* to mean playing an instrument. Therefore, the argument goes, the use of *psallō* in the New Testament indicates that God approves of instrumental music in New Testament worship.

That argument fails in light of careful examination. In fact, I would argue that the manner in which New Testament writers use *psallō* makes an extremely powerful case for a cappella music in the praise of God.

The Usage of Psallō

Psallō appears in the New Testament five times: "I will praise you among the Gentiles, and sing (*psallō*) to your name" (Rom 15:9). "I will sing praise (*psallō*) with my spirit, but I will sing (*psallō*) with my mind also" (1 Cor 14:15). "Do not get drunk with wine, for that is debauchery, but be filled with the Spirit, addressing one another in psalms and hymns and spiritual songs, singing and making melody (*psallō*) to the Lord with your heart" (Eph 5:18-19). "Is anyone cheerful? Let him sing praise (*psallō*)" (Js 5:13).

In classical Greek, *psallō* did mean the touching of a string. Aeschylus (525-456 BC), the well-known Greek playwright, used *psallō* for the plucking of a hair. Euripides (480-460 BC) used the word to mean the "twanging" of a bowstring. *Psallō* indicated the "twitching" of a carpenter's line so that it would leave a mark. For Plutarch *psallō* was the "plucking" on the strings of an instrument. That usage prevailed so that *psallō* came to mean touching the strings of an instrument opposed to using a pick.

Thus, the argument is this: Since *psallō* referred to the touching of an instrument's strings and Paul and James use *psallō*, God authorizes churches to use instrumental music in worship. The argument, however, fails under careful scrutiny.

Fallacies of the Argument

First, if God inspired James and John to use *psallō* to mean the playing of a string instrument, we must use stringed instruments in our praise to God. James uses *psallō* as the appropriate reaction of the cheerful. If I'm in my car and cheerful, I cannot sing unless I have a stringed instrument to play. Some might say my example is extreme, but if *psallō* means to play a stringed instrument, pray tell me how my joyful praise can be otherwise. Either *psallō* means to play a stringed instrument or it does not – we cannot have it both ways.

If we absolutely must use stringed instruments in our worship, what about small congregations without members able to play the harp or guitar? Has God placed upon them a burden they cannot bear? God does not place upon his people burdens they cannot lift (Acts 15:10). Again, if *psallō* means the playing of a stringed instrument, pray tell me how it can be otherwise.

Many of those advocating instrumental music on the use of *psallō* assert the word allows instrumental music but does not require its use. Notice, for example, what one scholar in the independent Christian Church had to say: "Psalmos (or its cognate verb psallo [*sic*]) is used to mean instrumental music, or a song played to musical accompaniment in the Greek Old Testament. . . . For this reason and others we believe that Paul's use of the term psalm shows that God approves the use of instrumental music in our teaching and admonishing. However, they do not establish that such music must be used at all times."[1] But, if *psallō* means to play an instrument, God has commanded it, and should we refuse to do so, we are sinning against God! It can be no other way.

Second, if *psallō* means to play a stringed instrument in the New Testament, we each must play a stringed instrument. Notice Ephesians 5:19 again: We are to be "addressing one another in psalms and hymns and spiritual songs, singing and making melody (*psallō*) to the Lord with your heart." Paul uses the plural participle; in short, each one of us would need to play a stringed instrument. Think about the implication: God would be commanding me to do something based upon musical talent!

I have absolutely no musical talent whatsoever. Zilch. Nada. Nothing. I tried to play the trombone in the school band. Dad had played the trombone and I wanted to be just like my dad. I was horrible! If God is commanding that I play a stringed instrument, he's requiring that I use that non-existent talent for his glory. Of course, God requires nothing that I cannot do. In the Parable of the Talents, we read that the master gave "to each according to his ability" (Matt 25:15).

---

[1] Wilbur Fields, *Philippians – Colossians – Philemon* in Bible Study Textbook Series (College Press: Joplin, MO: 1969), 224.

But, if God is requiring that I play a stringed instrument, he isn't giving me a requirement according to my ability – he's giving me a requirement far beyond my ability.

Third, if *psallō* authorizes instrumental music, the word's inspired use only authorizes stringed instruments. *Psallō* means to touch the strings. Therefore, any wind instrument is out; I couldn't use drums or a tambourine; I could not use an electronic keyboard. I could only use a stringed instrument. Furthermore, the piano would be out. Yes, I know that the piano has strings, but you do not touch them when you're playing. You hit keys that move hammers that touch the strings. *Psallō* means to touch the finger to the string. If I were using a guitar, I couldn't use a pick. I'd literally have to touch the strings; that is what the term means.

Fourth, those who affirm that *psallō* authorizes instrumental music overlook the fact that words change meanings. F. F. Bruce, a well-known evangelical scholar of the late 20th century, wrote, "Words are not static things, they change their meanings with the passage of time. Many words used in the A.V. no longer possess in current English the meanings they had in 1611."[2] We all know that words change meaning. Those of you who use the King James Version understand that "conversation" in the 1600s meant "manner of life" and today it means "manner of speaking."

The term *psallō* drastically changed its meaning over the course of time. E. A. Sophocles' *Greek Lexicon of the Roman and Byzantine Periods (From B.C. 146 to A.D. 1100)* defines *psallō* as "chant, sing religious hymns." The Septuagint, the Greek translation of the Old Testament completed about 250 years before Jesus, greatly influenced the New Testament's use of *psallō*. Some texts in the Septuagint clearly use *psallō* to mean playing on a stringed

---

[2] F. F. Bruce, ed., *Vine's Expository Dictionary of Old and New Testament Words* by W. E. Vine (Grand Rapids, MI: F. H. Revell Co., 1985), vi.

instrument: "Whenever the harmful spirit from God was upon Saul, David took the lyre and played (*psallō*) it with his hand" (1 Sam 16:23) and "Then a harmful spirit from the LORD came upon Saul, as he sat in his house with his spear in his hand. And David was playing (*psallō*) the lyre" (1 Sam 19:9). Notice that in both of these passages the context mentions the instrument.

In some passages the Septuagint clearly uses *psallō* to mean vocal praise. "My lips will shout for joy, when I sing praises (*psallō*) to you; my soul also, which you have redeemed. And my tongue will talk of your righteous help all the day long" (Ps 71:23-24). The idea here is clearly vocal music, for the text speaks of lips shouting for joy and the tongue talking of God's righteousness. "Sing to him, sing praises (*psallō*) to him; tell of all his wondrous works!" (Ps 105:2). The idea in this verse is clearly vocal praise, for the psalmist says that one is to "tell of all" God's works.

Some might claim that these two references do not demonstrate that *psallō* carried a vocal connotation in these passages. After all, one might say, "Someone could shout for joy with the lips while he played on an instrument." Such a claim overlooks the use of Hebrew parallelism. In Hebrew poetry, the second line often repeats the exact same idea in slightly different words. For example, notice Psalm 1:2: "His delight is in the law of the LORD, and on his law he meditates day and night." Delighting in the law of the LORD is the same thing as meditating on that law day and night. Therefore, in Psalm 71 shouting to the LORD for joy is the same thing as singing praises to God; in Psalm 105 singing praise to God is the same thing as telling of his wondrous works. Since one cannot shout to the LORD with one's lips by using an instrument and one cannot tell of God's wondrous works by using an instrument, *psallō* refers purely to vocal praise in these two Psalms.

The Greek construction in the Septuagint is quite important for New Testament usage. When *psallō* is used to refer to instrumental music, the typical construction is to use the preposition *en* (with/on) and put the instrument played in the dative case. That is, for example, the construction at 1 Samuel 19:9 where David plays upon his lyre to calm Saul's evil spirit.

However, when the Lord is mentioned as the one to whom the music is directed, the Lord is mentioned in the dative case without the preposition *en*. That becomes important as one looks at Ephesians 5:19. If Paul intended *psallō* to mean "to play," he has specified the instrument upon which the playing is to be done – the human heart. Paul's use of *psallō* cannot be used to advocate instrumental music in light of the term's use in the Septuagint.

Early Christians used *psallō* to indicate vocal praise. Clement of Alexandia, who lived at the end of the second century, uses a quite extensive musical vocabulary. Clement often uses *psallō* to introduce quotations from the Psalms. We would translate his words as "The Holy Spirit (or David) sings...." or "The Holy Spirit (or David) says in the Psalms...." Especially illustrative is this line from Clement: "This word sings (*psallō*) through David concerning our Lord, saying...."

In the third century, Origen wrote this in regard to 1 Corinthians 14:15: "For neither can our understanding pray, unless previously the Spirit prays, hearkening as it were to it, nor likewise can it sing (*psallō*) and hymn the Father in Christ with rhythm, melody, measure and harmony, unless the Spirit...first praise and hymn him." Our understanding cannot play on a musical instrument.

Why would the early Christians use *psallō* to refer to vocal praise if the New Testament means to play a stringed instrument? Someone might say, "Justin, the word simply changed meaning. These folks wrote 150-250 years after the time of the apostles and words can change meaning in less time than that." That's true.

However, do we Christians not typically use words in their biblical meaning? For example, when I mention

16

"baptism," I'm not talking about sprinkling some water on a baby's head. I'm not even talking about adult immersion to join the church. When I say "baptism," I am speaking – as the Bible does – of the immersion of a believing adult for the remission of sins. Nothing else is really baptism. If *psallō* in the New Testament mean to play an instrument, certainly those closest to the time of the apostles would have known that and would not have use *psallō* to mean vocal praise.

Those who know Greek best declare that *psallō* means vocal praise in the New Testament. W. E. Vine who produced the well-known *Expository Dictionary of New Testament Words*, said, "The word *psallō* originally meant to play a stringed instrument with the fingers, or to sing with the accompaniment of a harp. Later, however, and in the New Testament, it came to signify simply to praise without the accompaniment of an instrument."[3] Ralph Earle who wrote *Word Meanings in the New Testament*, says, "'Making melody' is one word in Greek, *psallontes*. The verb *psallō* meant first to strike the strings of a harp or lyre. Then it meant to 'strike up a tune.' Finally, the word meant 'to sing.'"[4]

The argument that *psallō* includes instrumental music also ignores the history of the early church. It is an undeniable fact that the earliest Christians did not use instrumental music. All church historians recognize this fact. If *psallō* meant to sing with accompaniment in the New Testament, why did the early Christians disobey that command?

As far as the patristic evidence goes, we McClintock and Strong noted:

> The Greeks as well as the Jews were wont to use instruments as accompaniments in their sacred

---

[3] W. E. Vine, *First Corinthians* (Grand Rapids, Mich: Zondervan, 1951), 191.
[4] Ralph H. Earle, *Word Meanings in the New Testament* (Peabody, Mass: Hendrickson Publishers, 1997), 333.

songs. The converts to Christianity accordingly must have been familiar with this mode of singing; yet it is generally believed that the primitive Christians failed to adopt the use of instrumental music in their religious worship. The word *psallein*, which the apostle uses in Eph. 5:19, has been taken by some critics to indicate that they sang with such accompaniments … But if this be the correct inference, it is strange indeed that neither Ambrose … nor … Basil … nor Chrysostom … in the noble encomiums which they severally pronounce upon music, make any mention of instrumental music. Basil, indeed, expressly condemns it as ministering only to the depraved passions of men … and [he] must have been led to this condemnation because some had gone astray and borrowed this practice from the heathen … The general introduction of instrumental music can certainly not be assigned to a date earlier than the 5th or 6th centuries.[5]

If as critics allege, *psallō* includes the use of instrumental music in worship, why did the early church – who knew the Greek language far better than modern scholars not use instrumental music in their worship?

Obviously, *psallō* does not have any reference to using instrumental music in the New Testament. There is, in fact, absolutely no authority for the use of instrumental music in the worship of the church. Let us resolve to honor God the way he has directed!

---

[5] McClintock, John & Strong, James Baker *Cyclopedia of Biblical, Theological, and Ecclesiastical Literature* Vol VI (Grand Rapids, MI: 1969), 759.

3

God Didn't Say I Can't

Music is quite powerful. Jamie Rouse walked into his Lynnville, Tennessee, high school on November 15, 1995, and killed a teacher and a student. When asked what drove him to kill, Rouse said his choice of music influenced his actions. He said, "I used to think, 'This ain't affecting me, you'd have to be weak-minded to let this stuff affect you,' and the whole time it affected me."

Martin Luther understood the power of music. He said, "The devil should not be allowed to keep all the best tunes for himself." Luther also said, "Music is a glorious gift of God, very like to theology. I would not part with my little gifts of music for anything in the world. We ought to teach the young this art, for it makes fine and clever people." Again, the famed Reformer said, "Next after theology, I give to music the highest place and the greatest honor."

God, because he knew the power of music, included music in the worship of the church. "Be filled with the Spirit, addressing one another in psalms and hymns and spiritual songs, singing and making melody to the Lord with your heart" (Eph 5:18-19). "Let the word of Christ dwell in you richly, teaching and admonishing one another in all wisdom, singing psalms and hymns and spiritual songs, with thankfulness in your hearts to God" (Col 3:16).

Several have rightfully pointed out through the years that the context of both of these passages is the Christian life, not the Christian worship assembly. Therefore, many have said that the New Testament says absolutely nothing about singing in the assembly. While it is true that the context of these passages is the Christian life, it is not true that the singing takes place privately.

Ephesians 5 speaks of "addressing one another" and Colossians 3 speaks of "teaching and admonishing one another." Such activities cannot take place in private, but they require the assembly. Further, the verbs are reflexive in Greek; therefore, the addressing and teaching take place simultaneously in the assembly.

But, must that singing be a cappella? One frequently heard argument in favor of instrumental music is that God doesn't say not to use the instrument. Whether God's silence on something allows or prohibits its use has been a subject of intense debate. Martin Luther, whom we quoted earlier and who was personally opposed to instrumental music, believed that if God did not specifically forbid a practice that practice was acceptable. Ulrich Zwingli, on the other hand, firmly believed that one could only do what God had specifically authorized him to do. Who was right?

First, we need to understand that some things are wrong even though the Bible says nothing about them. I cannot find a single word in Scripture that says I cannot view pornographic materials on the Internet. Yet, the activity is wrong, for God has given specific guidelines. "I say to you that everyone who looks at a woman with lustful intent has already committed adultery with her in his heart" (Mt 5:28). "Do not rebuke an older man but encourage him as you would a father, younger men as brothers, older women as mothers, younger women as sisters, in all purity" (1 Tm 5:1-2).

I cannot find a single word in Scripture that says the destruction of embryos for medical research is sinful. But again, God has given us guidelines that would prohibit Christians from participating in such. For example, we know that life begins at the point of conception: "If the woman has not defiled herself and is clean, then she shall be free and shall conceive *children*" (Num 5:28, emphasis mine); notice that it is children, not embryos, who are conceived. We dare not take human life: "Whoever sheds the blood of man, by man shall his blood be shed, for God made man in his own image" (Gen

9:6). Because life begins at conception and murder is unacceptable, embryos cannot rightfully be destroyed for medical research.

Can you imagine a Bible in which God told us everything that is right or wrong? The book would be so large it would be impossible to carry and even more impossible to know. What about the parts of the Bible that would make absolutely no sense to us because certain evil has yet to be invented? Just imagine what our first-century brethren would have thought if God needed specific instructions about Internet pornography or embryonic stem cell research! Because that evil wasn't available to them, they would certainly have been confused! Can you imagine how confused we might be if God spoke about evil that might be invented in the next 500 years? Yet, God has provided us with guidelines that shall stand for eternity.

Second, we also need to understand that specifics leave no wiggle room. The biblical principle is quite clear: when God says specifically what he wants, everything else is excluded (Num 20:7-13). We have always rightfully pointed to the pride Moses demonstrates in this narrative; as he lifts up the staff, he says, "Shall we bring water for you out of this rock?" (v 10). Notice, however, that additionally Moses does not do exactly what God has told him to do. Because God had said that Moses was to speak to the rock that excluded everything else.

In speaking of the superiority of Jesus to the angels, the author of Hebrews writes, "For to which of the angels did God ever say, 'You are my Son, today I have begotten you'? Or again, 'I will be to him a father, and he shall be to me a son'?" (Heb 1:5). Because God never said such to the angels, it was not so. Jesus is the unique Son of God, for he is the only One to Whom the Father ever said, "You are my Son."

About Jesus' superior priesthood, the author of Hebrews writes, "When there is a change in the priesthood, there is necessarily a change in the law as well. For the one of whom these things are spoken belonged to another tribe, from which no one has ever served at the altar. For it is evident that our Lord was descended from Judah, and in connection with that tribe Moses said *nothing* about priests" (Heb 7:12-14, emphasis added). God never said that someone from the tribe of Judah could not serve as a priest – not even once. But, when God said, "Priests shall come from Levi," he naturally excluded all other tribes.

Third, any law of exclusion only applies when there are specifics. You are tired after a long day at work, and you pull up in front of GoMart, hand your son some money and tell him to run in and get a gallon of milk. He comes back with a gallon of orange juice; he likes it better, he says. Are you going to be happy? Why not? You gave him specific instructions he disobeyed.

Likewise, God has specified singing as the type of music to be offered before him. It's obvious that God could have commanded instruments to be used as well – he did so in the Old Testament and musical instruments were known to the early Christians. But, when God says, "Here is what I want," he doesn't need to spell out everything he doesn't want.

So many stumble at this point. Scripture doesn't mention many things we use in modern worship – a church building, a pulpit, pews, a pitch pipe, songbooks, and the PowerPoint projector, for example. People will say, "Since God is silent on those things, what gives you the right to use them?" Understand that simply because something is not mentioned in Scripture as a part of worship does not make it wrong. But when God says, "Here is what I want," that excludes everything else. In other words, only when God is specific do exclusions apply.

Let's apply this "law of specifics" to two parts of our worship. Let's take preaching first. Nowhere in the New Testament, do I read of a pulpit or of using notes or of using PowerPoint. I can use those aides because they do not change

22

the act of preaching. Mechanical instruments of music, on the other hand, do change the act of singing.

But, what about having a play next Sunday morning instead of a sermon? Nowhere does God say I cannot do that. But, notice what God does want: "On the first day of the week, when we were gathered together to break bread, Paul talked with them, intending to depart on the next day, and he prolonged his speech until midnight" (Acts 20:7). The specific of a speech excludes everything else; God nowhere, however, specified the form the sermon must take – expository, topical, textual, narrative – and he nowhere specified what visual aids can or cannot be used – bedsheets (for those who remember those old sermons), PowerPoint. Because God has not specified the form, I may utilize what form I choose as long as it does not change the act of preaching.

Let's take the Lord's Supper. Nowhere in the New Testament do I read of using communion trays or even having men pass the emblems through the assembly. But, using trays and having our brethren serve us doesn't change the act of the Lord's Supper. But, what if next Lord's Day we wanted Twinkies and Coca-Cola? Jesus used unleavened bread and fruit of the vine. Everything else, therefore, is excluded.

If God has simply said, "Make music," we would be free to use any kind of music we wanted in our worship. However, God specified singing. Therefore, singing is the only thing I have a right to do.

A direct corollary of the "law of specifics" is that we are not to add to Scripture. "You shall not add to the word that I command you, nor take from it, that you may keep the commandments of the LORD your God that I command you" (Deut 4:2). "Do not add to his words, lest he rebuke you and you be found a liar" (Prov 30:6). "I warn everyone who hears the words of the prophecy of this book: if anyone adds to them, God will add to him the plagues described in this book, and if anyone takes away from the words of the book of this prophecy, God will take away his share in the tree of life and in the holy city, which are described in this book" (Rev 22:18-19).

When God has been specific, we dare not think that we humans can improve on what God has said. Let us honor God in the way that we worship!

4

My Aid

In 1860, L. L. Pinkerton was the preacher for the church at Midway, Kentucky. Pinkerton complained that the church's singing was so bad that it would scare the rats out of the church building. Thus, the melodeon was introduced in the church. Notice carefully that Pinkerton wanted that melodeon because the church's singing was deplorable.

Many heirs of the Restoration have argued that the instrument is an aid since Pinkerton first made that argument at Midway. There isn't a one of us who hasn't worshiped with a congregation where we found the singing much less than desirable. For aesthetic purposes, an instrument would have been highly desirable in such circumstances. But, is it proper to use the instrument as an aid?

This Argument Misunderstands the Use of Musical Instruments in the Old Testament

The idea that instrumental music can be an aid to worship overlooks two very important principles from Old Testament worship.

One: Instrumental music in the Old Testament was worship, not simply an aid. "The whole assembly worshiped, and the singers sang, and the trumpeters sounded" (2 Chr 26:28) – The trumpeters were not aiding the singing; their blowing on the trumpet was worship in and of itself.

The Levites, thirty years old and upward, were numbered, and the total was 38,000 men. 'Twenty-four thousand of these," David said, "shall have charge of the work in the house of the LORD, 6,000 shall be officers and judges, 4,000 gatekeepers, and 4,000 shall offer praise to the LORD with the instrumentals that I have made for praise" (1 Chr 23:3-5).

Four thousand were not going to accompany singing. Instead, they were going to offer praise to God with their instruments. "The priests stood at their posts; the Levites also, with the instruments for music to the LORD that King David had made for giving thanks to the LORD" (2 Chr 7:6) – David didn't make these instruments to accompany the praise of God; these instruments themselves were for the praise of God.

> Praise him with trumpet sound;
> praise him with lute and harp!
> Praise him with tambourine and dance;
> praise him with strings and pipe!
> Praise him with sounding cymbals;
> praise him with loud clashing cymbals! (Ps 150:3-5)

We understand that the Old Testament is no longer binding on us today, however: There is an important principle at work here – Instrumental music in the Old Covenant wasn't an aid to worship. Instrumental music wasn't used under the Law of Moses because it helped the Israelites sound better – The playing of instruments was in and of itself worship.

Two: God commanded instrumental music in the Old Testament. Hezekiah "stationed the Levites in the house of the LORD with cymbals, harps, and lyres, according to the commandment of David and of Gad the king's seer and of Nathan the prophet, for the commandment was from the LORD through his prophets" (2 Chr 26:25).

> Sing aloud to God our strength;
> shout for joy to the God of Jacob!

26

Raise a song; sound the tambourine,
the sweet lyre with the harp.
Blow the trumpet at the new moon,
at the full moon, on our feast day.

For it is a statute for Israel,
a rule of the God of Jacob (Ps 81:1-4)

These principles from the Old Testament establish that the instrument is far more than an aid to worship – it is worship.

An aid simply assists someone in fulfilling a task. For example, glasses can help one see, a cane can aid someone's walking, or a hearing aid can assist one's hearing. Someone who is wearing glasses is still seeing, someone who uses a cane is still walking, and someone using a hearing aid is still hearing.

But, in the Old Testament the instrument was actually a way that the Israelites worshiped God. It is inconsistent with biblical teaching to declare that singing is simply an aid in worship. Someone might want to be more consistent with the Old Testament principle and declare that instrumental music today isn't being used as an aid but it is being used as worship.

If someone declares that instrumental music today is part of our worship to God, he would only partially be consistent with the Old Testament principle. Granted, he would no longer be arguing that the instrument is an aid. However, instrumental music was commanded in the Old Testament. God was also very, very specific in what instruments were to be used, and the Israelites were only permitted to use the instruments God had commanded.

If God commanded instruments in the Old Testament and commanded specific instruments in the Old Testament, doesn't it stand to reason that had God wanted instrumental music in the church he would have commanded it?

27

This Argument Misunderstands the Nature of Worship

Worship is not about man; worship is about God. "The hour is coming, and is now here, when the true worshipers will worship the Father in spirit and truth, for the Father is seeking such people to worship him" (Jn 4:23). The Father isn't seeking people to come and worship him who like a particular aesthetic style; he isn't seeking people to worship him who can sing well. The Father seeks people to worship him "in spirit and truth." Worship must be the way God wants, not the way I want.

When John saw the glorified Christ, the four living creatures and the twenty-four elders fell before him and sang a new song:

> Worthy are you to take the scroll
>   and to open its seals,
> for you were slain, and by your blood you ransomed people for God
>   from every tribe and language and people and nation,
> and you have made them a kingdom and priests to our God,
>   and they shall reign on the earth (Rev 5:9-10).

The "new song" is interesting in the way it presents Christ's work of salvation. Humans are mentioned throughout this hymn: we have been ransomed, made kingly priests, and we shall reign on the earth. However, humans are far from the focus of this praise. It is the work of Christ that is praised: "You were slain," "By your blood you ransomed," "You have made them a kingdom and priests." These heavenly beings do speak of our salvation, but the focus is entirely on Christ, not on those who have been redeemed. Our praise needs to center

28

on our God, not on us!

Paul speaks of pagans who became more interested in themselves than in God:

> Although they knew God, they did not honor him as God or give thanks to him, but they became futile in their thinking, and their foolish hearts were darkened. Claiming to be wise, they became fools, and exchanged the glory of the immortal God for images resembling mortal man and birds and animals and creeping things (Rom 1:21-23).

Instead of honoring God as Creator, these pagans did what seemed best to them.

God is the only appropriate object of worship. When John fell down at the feet of the angel who had shown him the Revelation, the angel said, "You must not do that! I am a fellow servant with you and your brothers who hold to the testimony of Jesus. Worship God" (Rev 19:10). When Satan attempted to get Jesus to worship him, the Lord replied, "Be gone, Satan! For it is written, 'You shall worship the Lord your God and him only shall you serve'" (Mt 4:10). When I do anything that takes the focus off God and on me, I'm not worshiping properly.

Saying that I need an instrument for an aid greatly takes the focus off God and puts it on me. Why is it that I need an aid to sing? Someone will say, "Because it sounds better."

To whom? Does it sound better to me or does it sound better to God? We dare not forget that we are not the audience! God is the audience. Worship is about God!

There is nothing at all wrong with singing the best that we can. In fact, I believe that we need to sing to the best of our ability and bring our absolute best to God. God has always required the best and we dare not give him anything but the best. However, we dare not get to wrapped up in how worship pleases us – we need to be wrapped up in how worship pleases

God.

This Argument Misunderstands the Nature of an Aid

An "aid," by definition, is something that helps one fulfill the purpose of a task. The Powerpoint is helping me fulfill the purpose of teaching by allowing a visual as well as an auditory stimulus. Communion trays help us fulfill the purpose of the Lord's Supper by making sure everyone in the congregation is served.

However, instrumental music has nothing to do with the purpose for which we sing. We sing in order to praise God: "I will praise you among the Gentiles, and sing to your name" (Rom 15:9). How can an instrument help me praise the name of God any better? The author of Hebrews informs us that our praise to God is the fruit of our lips: "Through him then let us continually offer up a sacrifice of praise to God, that is, the fruit of lips that acknowledge his name" (Heb 13:15). There is no conceivable way that an instrument can assist me in giving to God the fruit of my lips and acknowledging his name.

Singing is a way that we teach one another. "Let the word of Christ dwell in you richly, teaching and admonishing one another in all wisdom, singing psalms and hymns and spiritual songs, with thankfulness in your hearts to God" (Col 3:16). An instrument cannot teach me a single thing. In fact, when I've been places where the instrument seemed to be an impediment to teaching; it is often difficult, if not impossible, to hear the words for the banging of the instrument.

Using a mechanical instrument in worship does not assist the singing as we teach one another and lift our voices in praise to the holy God.

This Argument Misunderstands Genetic Authority

Aids are used in much of our work in the church. This

pulpit assists me by allowing me a place to rest my notes and Bible. The pews help you by providing a place to sit during worship. The church building aids us all by furnishing a place to worship.

When God gives a command, we are free to use whatever is necessary to carry out that command. For example, when God told Noah to build the ark, Noah was free to use whatever was necessary to build the ark without changing the nature of the command (Gen 6:14-16).

If Noah wanted to obey God, he had no choice in many of the particulars. He was to build the ark of gopher wood – nothing else. He was to make it to its exact specifications – not a cubit higher or lower, not an extra deck, or not an extra window.

However, what tools did Noah need to complete the ark's construction? Because God had not specified the tools he was to use, Noah was free to do what seemed best to him.

When Jesus gave the Great Commission, he left many particulars up to his disciples. "Go . . . and make disciples of all nations, baptizing them in the name of the Father and of the Son and of the Holy Spirit" (Matt 28:19). We are to go and make disciples of all nations, but Jesus didn't tell us how to go. Paul went by boat, he walked, the Holy Spirit caught Philip and carried him to Azotus after the eunuch's conversion.

The important thing to notice is that regardless of what tools Noah used to construct the ark, he didn't change the nature of the ark; regardless of what tools we use to preach the Word throughout the world, we aren't changing the nature of the Gospel.

Some might well say that an instrument doesn't really change the nature of singing. Or, they might say, it doesn't change it enough to preclude the use of the instrument. Oh, contraire! Instrumental music and vocal music are different kinds of music. Someone might say that the distinction between instrumental and vocal music is a man-made distinction. No, I can find that distinction in Scripture. "The whole assembly worshiped, and the singers sang, and the trumpeters sounded" (2 Chr 29:28). A distinction is made in that passage between singing and playing the trumpet. "The song was raised, with trumpets and cymbals and other musical instruments, in praise to the LORD" (2 Chr 5:13). Notice that we are told the song was accompanied by musical instruments.

Let us commit ourselves to never using an aid that harms, rather than helps, the praise of God.

5

Instrumental Music in the Old Testament

There is an old story about a preacher who was standing outside a church building on a Sunday morning. A congregant approached the door of the church building with a bull. The preacher asked what the man was going to do with the bull. "I'm going to sacrifice it in worship this morning," the man said. The preacher replied, "You can't do that." "But, it's in the Old Testament," the man said. "Well," the preacher said, "the Old Testament has been abolished – you can't do that."

Another person arrived at the church with a bowl full of incense. Again, the preacher said, "What are you going to do with this incense?" "Well, I'm going to offer it with my prayers as Moses instructed." "You can't do that," said the preacher. "But, it's in the Old Testament," the man declared. "Well," declared the preacher, the Old Testament has been abolished – you can't do that."

Another person came to the building with a piano. "What are you going to do with that?" asked the preacher. "I'm going to play it with our singing this morning because David used a harp in the Old Testament." "Okay," responded the preacher, "bring it right on in."

Obviously, that story is apocryphal, and I don't think that any of our good friends caught up in the error of instrumental music stop to think of the inconsistency the issue creates. There are very few denominations that use incense, candles, bowls for washing, and the like in their worship, yet there are many who use instrumental music based, in part, on its use in the Old Testament. There are no denominations –

mainstream denominations, at least – of which I am aware that use animal sacrifices in their worship.

The problem is, of course, that the Old Testament, with all of its ceremonial regulations, has been fulfilled in Jesus and removed at his cross. "When there is a change in the priesthood, there is necessarily a change in the law as well" (Heb 7:12). The Law had been to be changed in order for Jesus to serve as our High Priest. One from the tribe of Judah could never serve as a priest under the Old Testament: "It is evident that our Lord was descended from Judah, and in connection with that tribe Moses said nothing about priests" (Heb 7:14).

"In speaking of a new covenant, he makes the first one obsolete. And what is becoming obsolete and growing old is ready to vanish away" (Heb 8:13). The former covenant has vanished away. We can, therefore, not go back to the Old Testament as our standard of faith and practice.

Because Jesus' death at Golgotha removed the Old Covenant as God's will for man, we cannot use the Old Testament to know how to worship acceptably. However, we recognize that the Old Testament often has principles which apply in any age – e.g., God is the Creator, men are made in God's image, God has always expected people to follow his will, and God punishes disobedience. Therefore, we will look to the Old Testament for principles which apply to the New Testament about instrumental music.

What does the Old Testament Say about Instrumental Music?

I have heard many brethren say that instrumental music in the Old Testament was never commanded by God, that it was an allowance to the hardness of hearts, something like divorce (cf. Matt 19:8). I've always found it quite odd that brethren would say that the use of instrumental music in the Old Testament was a concession on God's part when he told people to use such music at set times (God regulated, but never commanded, divorce). I believe some brethren have feared that saying God commanded instrumental music in the Old Testament would leave some wiggle room to say that it was allowed in the New Testament. However, God commanded much under the Old Testament which is no longer in effect today: circumcision, animal sacrifices, annual pilgrimages to Jerusalem, and the dedication of the firstborn, just for example.

God absolutely commanded instrumental music in the Old Testament and a failure to use instrumental music would have been a sin. You might be thinking the same thing I've thought for years: "Whether or not instrumental music was commanded or a concession to the weakness of flesh is a moot point, for God hasn't authorized it in the New Testament." I believe firmly that God never authorized musical instruments for his worship in the New Testament, and I believe that their use is sinful. However, I also believe that the Old Testament commands to use instrumental music have serious implications for New Testament worship.

God did command instrumental music in the Old Testament. God commanded Moses to use the trumpet in the tabernacle worship (Num 10:1-10). God not only commanded Moses to use these musical instruments in the tabernacle, but he also instructed Moses about how to construct them: "Make two silver trumpets. Of hammered work you shall make them, and you shall use them for summoning the congregation and for breaking camp" (Num 10:2). What if Moses had hammered three trumpets to use in worship? Would the Lord have been pleased if Moses had made these trumpets out of gold or some other material?

Only priests could blow these trumpets: "The sons of Aaron, the priests, shall blow the trumpets. The trumpets shall be to you for a perpetual statute throughout your generations" (Num 10:8). What if Moses had blown the trumpets? What if a descendent of Judah, as was the Lord Jesus, had blown the trumpets?

Those two trumpets were the only instruments ever

authorized for use in tabernacle worship, and until the time of David the two trumpets were the only musical instruments used in public worship. God, however, revealed to David authorization to begin using other musical instruments (1 Chr 16:5-6). David said about the Levites whom he had counted: "4,000 [are] gatekeepers, and 4,000 shall offer praises to the Lord with the instruments that *I have made* for praise" (1 Chron 23:5). The priests played musical instruments according to the *commandment* of David (Ezra 3:10; Neh 12:36).

Why did David bring these instruments into the worship at the temple? Maybe David, as a musician, simply liked these instruments. Not so (2 Chr 29:25-26). David did not introduce musical instruments because he liked them or because he wanted to, but because God told him to do so. Thus, when we read that people were following the command of David or using David's musical instruments, they were following the commandment of God.

What Should We Learn about Instrumental Music in the Old Testament?

In worship, God never left instrumental music to the devices of man. There have been several who have said that God doesn't really care if we use instruments or not. There have been many of our brethren who have argued that if God had simply said in the New Testament, "Make music," that we would be free to worship however we wanted. Quite honestly, I don't think either of those viewpoints totally captures what we learn from the Old Testament: God placed instrumental music under his authority – he told Moses precisely how many silver horns to make and he told David precisely what instruments to bring into the temple. Neither Moses nor David was free to use whatever instruments he desired in worship.

That principle, in my view, speaks volumes when we come to the New Testament where instrumental music in worship is never mentioned. In the Old Testament, God said, "Here's the instrument you are to use and here's how you are to use it." But, when we come to the New Testament, God never says that we are to use a mechanical instrument, but we are to use the instrument of our hearts (Eph 5:19).

God never authorized talented musicians to play the musical instruments in the Old Testament. The priests were to blow the trumpets in the tabernacle and Levites were to play the instruments in the temple. Because the priesthood has been abolished, there is no special class of priests separated from the rest of the people (1 Pet 2:5). All Christians are priests, and the major function of priests has always been to offer sacrifices to God.

As priests our function is to offer spiritual sacrifices and worship to God. Instead of having one or two people playing for everyone else, we all play on the instrument of our own hearts as we sing – We're to address "one another in psalms and hymns and spiritual songs, singing and making melody to the Lord with [our] heart[s]" (Eph 5:19).

Since God commanded specific instruments in the Old Testament, if he wanted them in the New Testament, doesn't it stand to reason that he would tell us precisely what he wanted now?

In fact, God has told us precisely what instrument he wants in this era – the human heart. We're to make "melody to the Lord with [our] heart[s]" (Eph 5:19). No silver trumpet. No lyre. No special instruments being played by a class of priests. The heart. Let us play our hearts in the worship of God and lift up our voices in his praise!

6

Instrumental Music in Heaven

I have often heard the use of instrumental music in heaven authorizes the use of instruments in worship on earth. Not long ago, I heard a new twist to that argument: A gentleman told me in all seriousness that the fact the archangel will blow the trumpet of God when Jesus returns (1 Thess 4:16) authorizes instrumental music in modern worship.[1] I told this gentleman that I honestly believed he had a valid point. I asked him if he would kindly let me know when he gets that archangel with that trumpet in the church building where he worships, and I'd be happy to sing while the archangel blows his trumpet.

My friend's idea has many difficulties. First, I must mention that nowhere do we read the angel will blow the trumpet in heaven – granted, that splits hairs and chases an unhelpful rabbit (plus, I do believe the implication in the text is that the angel will blow the trumpet). Second, and far more serious, is that the trumpet has nothing to do with the praise of Jehovah God – the trumpet is used to raise the dead. It would be an immense stretch to use the blaring trumpet to authorize instrumental music in the church's worship.

The Use of Instrumental Music in Heaven

We do read of instrumental music being used in heaven.

---

[1] The text nowhere specifically says that the archangel will blow the trumpet, but a careful reading of the text strongly implies that he will.

> When [the Lamb] had taken the scroll, the four
> living creatures and the twenty-four elders fell down
> before the Lamb, each holding a harp, and golden
> bowls full of incense, which are the prayers of the
> saints. And they sang a new song. . . . (Rev 5:8-9).

Again,

> I saw what appeared to be a sea of glass mingled
> with fire – and also those who had conquered the
> beast and its image and the number of its name,
> standing beside the sea of glass with harps of God in
> their hands. And they sing the song of Moses, the
> servant of God, and the song of the Lamb
> (Rev 15:2-3).

Some opponents might wish to point out that John never actually says the elders, living creatures, or the conquerors ever used the harps; he simply says that they held the harps and sang. Talk about splitting hairs! John mentions the harps and singing in such close proximity, there can really be no doubt but that the harps were played. Yes, John, inspired of the Spirit, mentions instrumental music in heaven.

As you read the Revelation, you will also read of angels with trumpets. "I saw the seven angels who stand before God, and seven trumpets were given to them" (Rev 8:2). Who gave the angels their trumpets? They stand before God and the angels will bring forth the judgment of God; therefore, God obviously gave them their trumpets.

The angels blow their trumpets and the wrath of God comes upon the sinful world of the Roman Empire. Using the angels as authority to use instrumental music in the modern church seems odd for two reasons: **One:** The angels do not blow their trumpets in the praise of God. Granted, God is glorified by the judgment which follows the sounding of the trumpets, but the angels' blowing of the trumpets is not directly praise of God. **Two:** The angels blow their trumpets to bring the judgment of God upon the world. Why would I wish to justify the use of instrumental music on the basis of divine judgment? I'd personally prefer to find a better argument than that.

Why Does Instrumental Music in Heaven Not Authorize Instrumental Music on Earth?

Several factors preclude the use of instrumental music in New Testament worship based on the use of harps in the Revelation.

One: Jesus gave John the Revelation in symbols – a dragon knocks stars down from heaven, an eagle flies in the sky and cries out with a loud voice, a beast comes out of the sea and another comes out of the land. Surely, no one would seek to justify such practices in modern worship.

Two: Much that is pictured as being in heaven in Revelation cannot or is not used in modern worship. We find an altar with incense being offered before the throne of God, but churches don't have altars before God's throne with angels offering incense. A sea of glass and four living beings and twenty-four elders and a woman in travail and temples being measured are not part of modern worship. Why choose one element of heavenly praise and seek to make it normative for the worship of the New Testament church?

Three: The reality of heaven does not match the reality of earth. Marriage does not exist in heaven (Matt 22:30), but marriage is a reality in this fallen world. Tears exist on earth; tears shall not exist in heaven (Rev 21:4). Heaven shall be a totally different experience than what we presently know.

Four: If the Revelation does authorize instrumental music in worship, only two instruments are authorized – the trumpet and the harp. I would not have the right to add a piano

41

or a guitar or a drum or any other instrument. Someone might object and say that I'm being far too restrictive in reading this text, but the inspired pen warns us to add nothing to "the words of the prophecy of this book" (Rev 22:18). To keep from adding to the words of the prophecy John received, I cannot add instruments not used in that prophecy.

The instruments of heaven do not authorize the use of instrumental music on earth. But, I certainly look forward to the day that I hear those instruments – that day I am in the presence of the Almighty God and I worship him for an eternity.

Also by the Author

Two Wonders: Studies in the Death and Resurrection of Jesus Christ

Selected Sermons
Messages from the Manger: Studies for Christmas

For more information, visit

http://www.drjustinimelsr.com

About the Author

Dr. Justin Imel is married to the former Tammy McKinney; the Imels have two children, RJ and Wilson. Dr. Imel has served churches of Christ in Kentucky, West Virginia, Tennessee, and Virginia. He has taught at Appalachian Bible Institute, Ohio Valley University, and Heritage Christian University. Dr. Imel holds a Doctor of Ministry in Church Leadership and Church Growth from Amridge University in Montgomery, Alabama. The Imels make their home in Roanoke, Virginia, with their puppy, Bacon.

www.ingramcontent.com/pod-product-compliance
Lightning Source LLC
Chambersburg PA
CBHW060623030426
42337CB00018B/3160